D1442932

# MONSTERS

## BY DAVID SCHACH

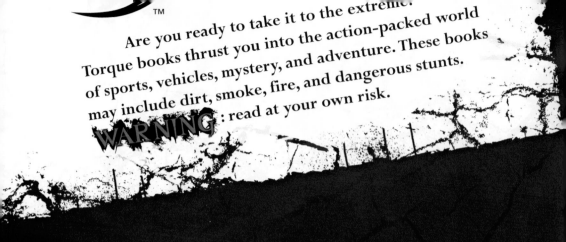

TM

Are you ready to take it to the extreme?
Torque books thrust you into the action-packed world
of sports, vehicles, mystery, and adventure. These books
may include dirt, smoke, fire, and dangerous stunts.

WARNING: read at your own risk.

Library of Congress Cataloging-in-Publication Data

Schach, David.
 Sea monsters / by David Schach.
   p. cm. -- (Torque. The unexplained)
 Includes bibliographical references and index.
 Summary: "Engaging images accompany information about sea monsters. The combination of high-
interest subject matter and light text is intended for students in grades 3 through 7"--Provided by
publisher.
 ISBN 978-1-60014-644-2 (hardcover : alk. paper)
 1. Sea monsters--Juvenile literature.  I. Title.
QL89.2.S4S34 2011
591.77--dc22

                                    2011002255

This edition first published in 2012 by Bellwether Media, Inc.

Printed in the United States of America, North Mankato, MN.

080111   1187

# CONTENTS

# CHAPTER 1

# TERROR FROM THE DEEP

It is a warm, sunny day. The captain of a ship watches the sea. The water is calm. Suddenly, a sailor yells, "Man overboard!" He has spotted a man in the water. The crew rushes to rescue him. The man has been on a small raft in the water for more than a day. The crew gives the man water to drink. He then tells them how his ship sank.

"I was working on a small ship," he says. "One morning, I awoke to screams coming from the **deck**. I ran out of my cabin to see the men fighting giant **tentacles**. Then I was knocked into the water. I swam for my life. I could only watch as the beast dragged the ship beneath the waves."

# LUSC LURKING

Modern sailors have reported a 200-foot (61-meter) monster called Lusca in the Caribbean Sea. Many people think Lusca is a kind of giant octopus.

A few sailors look nervously at the water. Some say that they have seen similar sea monsters. Others think the man is having **delusions**. They don't believe his story. Do you?

# CHAPTER 2

# WHAT ARE SEA MONSTERS?

Stories of sea monsters have spread for thousands of years. Almost every culture that traveled by sea had its own tales. The **ancient** Greeks believed that the seas were full of dangerous creatures. They wrote about many kinds of sea dragons and sea serpents. Other cultures told of the **Leviathan** and giant **kraken**. Sailors reported that **mermaids** often tried to lure them into the water.

Sailors still report seeing giant squids and octopuses. A few say these creatures use tentacles to pull ships underwater. Some reports describe man-eating sharks and boat-ramming whales. Could these animals have inspired past legends?

HERE BE DRAGONS

Much of the world was unexplored when people began making maps. Mapmakers often drew sea monsters on unknown parts of the sea. They wrote "Here Be Dragons" as a warning to sailors.

# FAMOUS SEA MONSTERS

## Description

This sea monster of Greek legend sucks in huge amounts of water. It creates a whirlpool that can sink ships.

Norse legend tells of these giant sea monsters that sink ships, destroy cities, and eat people.

Some cultures believe that this massive sea serpent is the guardian of darkness and evil.

A large beast has been reported in the water of Scotland's Loch Ness since the 1960s.

This creature is said to swim in the waters of the Caribbean. Sailors have said it looks like a giant octopus.

These creatures are reported to have the upper body of a woman and the tail of a fish.

This strange, fish-like monster is reported to look like a person wearing a robe. Many people think this creature is actually a giant squid.

# CHAPTER 3

# SEARCHING FOR ANSWERS

manatee

**M**any **theories** try to explain sea
monster reports. One theory is that
sailors had delusions after months
at sea. They didn't always get the nutrients their
bodies needed. They might have mistaken whales,
sharks, and squids for monsters. Some people
think seals, dolphins, and **manatees** could have
been seen as mermaids.

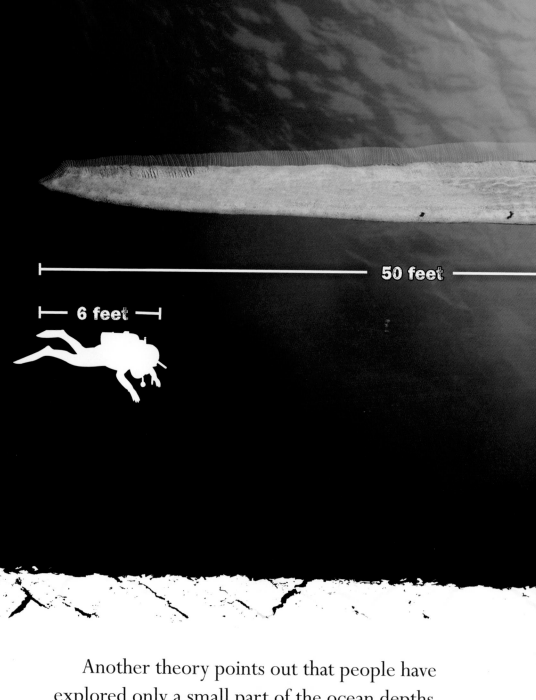

50 feet

6 feet

Another theory points out that people have explored only a small part of the ocean depths. The unexplored areas could hold rarely seen animals. These animals could look like sea monsters of legend.

oarfish

One such animal is the oarfish. It can grow to be 50 feet (15 meters) long and weigh up to 600 pounds (272 kilograms). Its appearance could have inspired tales of serpents and dragons.

A third theory is that sea monsters were once real but are now **extinct**. People point to **fossils** of sea creatures that have been found in many parts of the world.

This is the skeleton of an extinct ocean predator known as the mosasaur. Mosasaurs were large sea lizards that lived millions of years ago. They were able to swallow prey whole with their snake-like jaws!

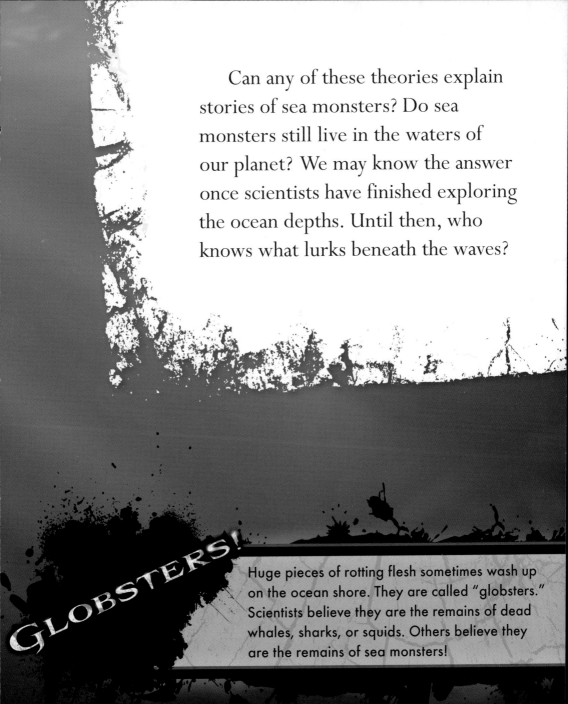

Can any of these theories explain stories of sea monsters? Do sea monsters still live in the waters of our planet? We may know the answer once scientists have finished exploring the ocean depths. Until then, who knows what lurks beneath the waves?

GLOBSTERS!

Huge pieces of rotting flesh sometimes wash up on the ocean shore. They are called "globsters." Scientists believe they are the remains of dead whales, sharks, or squids. Others believe they are the remains of sea monsters!

# GLOSSARY

**ancient**—existing more than 1,500 years ago

**deck**—the flat level of a ship where most of the crew works

**delusions**—beliefs that are not based on fact; some sailors have had delusions about sea monsters.

**extinct**—no longer living

**fossils**—the remains of plants or animals from long ago

**kraken**—giant sea monsters of Norse legend

**Leviathan**—a huge, legendary sea serpent; some cultures believe the Leviathan to be the guardian of darkness and evil.

**manatees**—large marine mammals that live off the coasts of North and South America

**mermaids**—creatures reported to have the head and body of a woman and the tail of a fish

**tentacles**—long, flexible, arm-like body parts; octopuses, squids, and other sea creatures have tentacles.

**theories**—ideas that try to explain why something exists or happens

# TO LEARN MORE

## AT THE LIBRARY

Beaumont, Steve. *Drawing the Kraken and Other Sea Monsters*. New York, N.Y.: PowerKids Press, 2011.

Harrison, Paul. *Sea Monsters*. New York, N.Y.: PowerKids Press, 2008.

Schach, David. *The Loch Ness Monster*. Minneapolis, Minn.: Bellwether Media, 2010.

## ON THE WEB

Learning more about sea monsters is as easy as 1, 2, 3.

1. Go to www.factsurfer.com.

2. Enter "sea monsters" into the search box.

3. Click the "Surf" button and you will see a list of related Web sites.

With factsurfer.com, finding more information

# INDEX